Cardinals Splendor

"GO CARDS!"

jo ann kargus

Reedy Press
PO Box 5131
St. Louis, MO 63139, USA
www.reedypress.com

ISBN: 9781681061207

Printed in the United States of America
17 18 19 20 21   5 4 3 2 1

Cardinals Splendor

By Jo Ann Kargus

REEDY PRESS

THIS IS HOW IT STARTS

Take me out to the
Ball Game
TAKE ME OUT TO THE
CROWD
buy me some
peanuts and cracker jack
I DON'T CARE IF I EVER GET BACK
LET ME ROOT! ROOT! ROOT!
FOR THE
"Cardinals"
IF THEY DON'T WIN IT'S A SHAME
For it's 1-2-3 strikes you're out!
At the old Ball Game!

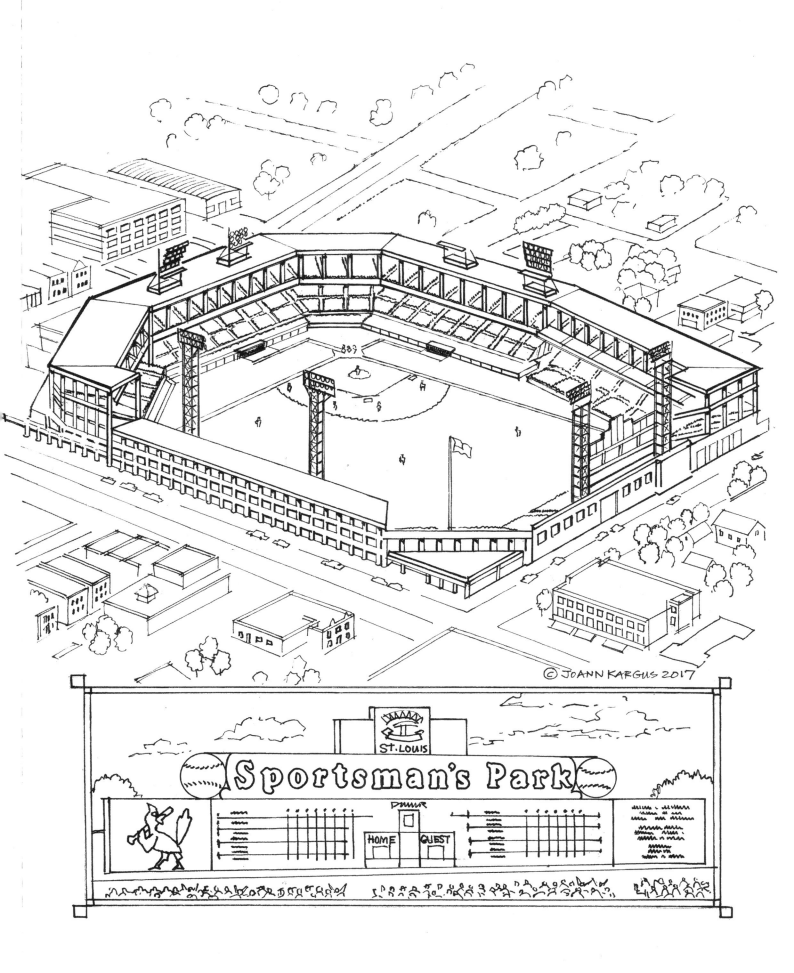

© JOANN KARGUS 2017

ST. LOUIS

Sportsman's Park

HOME   GUEST

BUSCH STADIUM

1966-2005

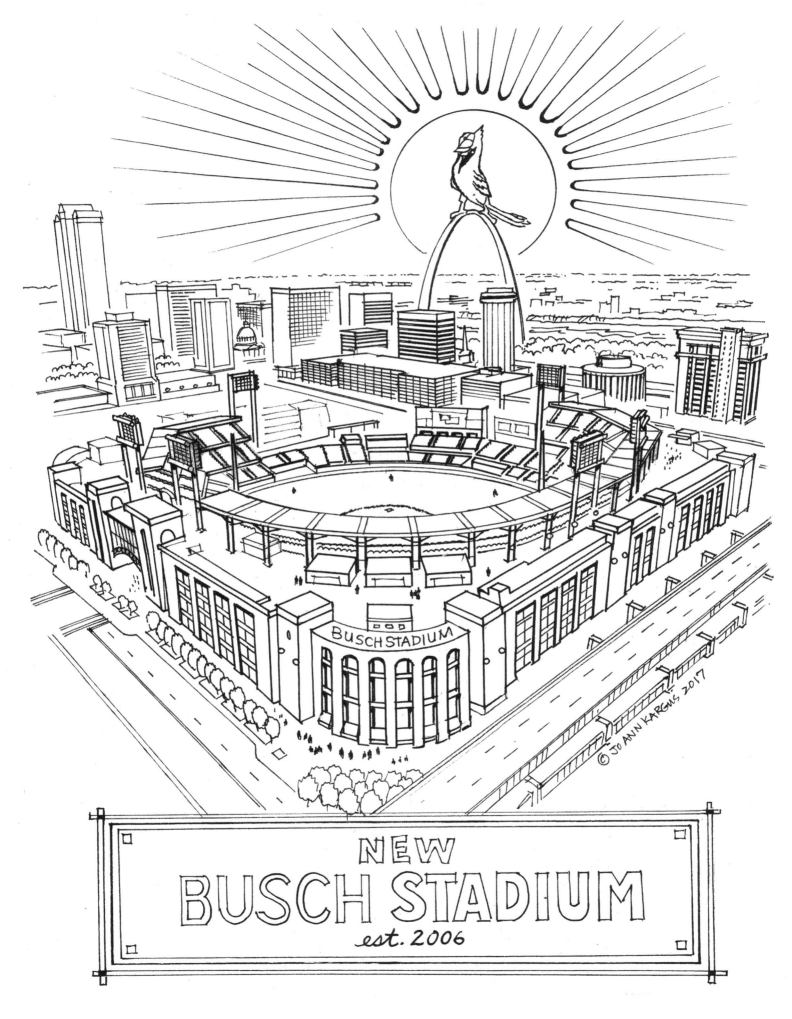

BUSCH STADIUM

© JO ANN KARGUS 2017

NEW
BUSCH STADIUM
est. 2006

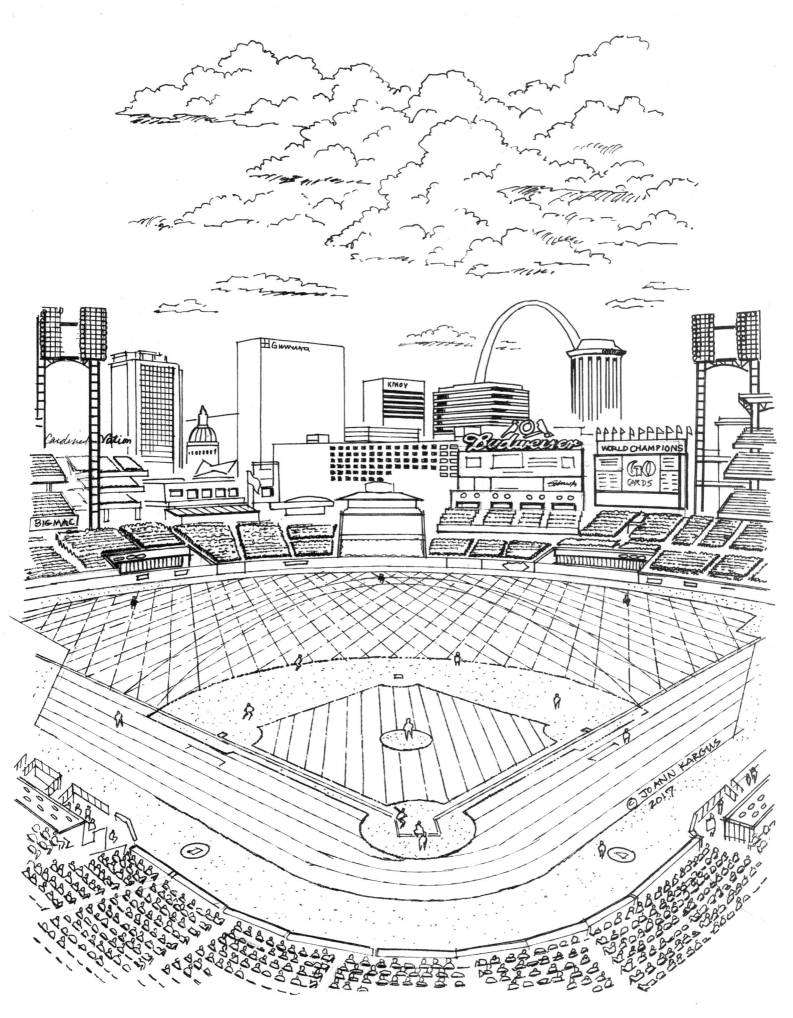

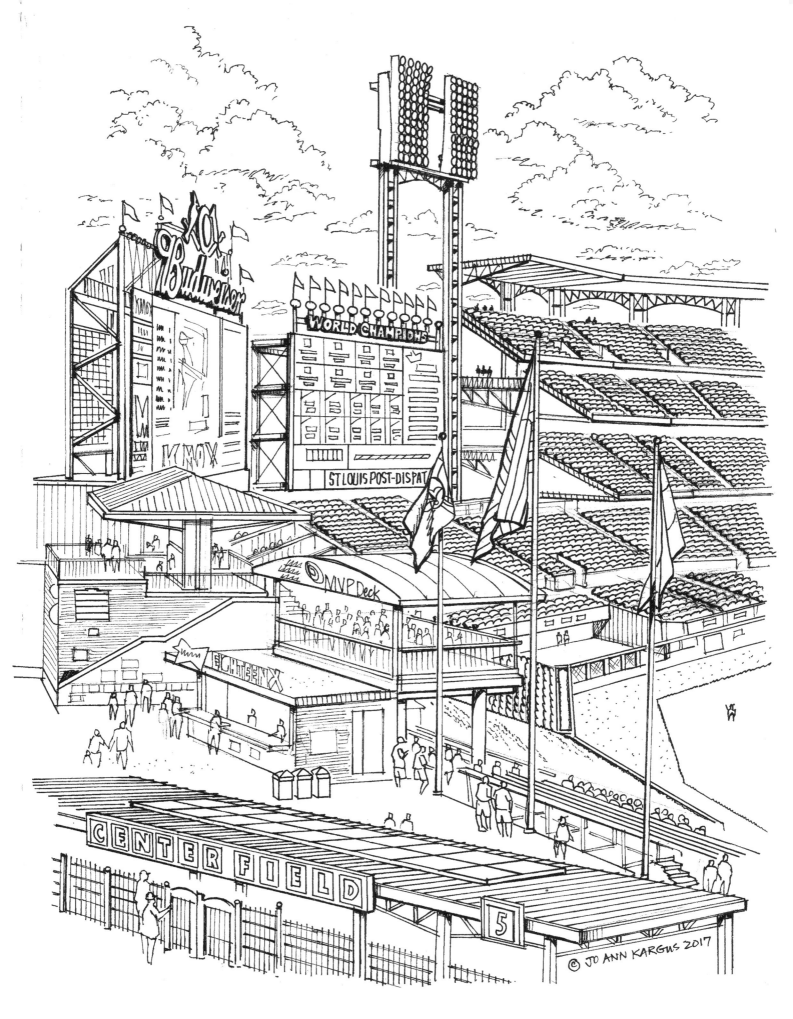

MUSIAL
"...HERE STANDS
BASEBALL'S PERFECT WARRIOR"
"...HERE STANDS
BASEBALL'S PERFECT KNIGHT"

JOANN KARGUS
2017

the Statues...

BROCK

MUSIAL

DEAN

SLAUGHTER

HORNSBY

SISLER

BELL

SCHOENDIENST

SMITH

GIBSON

© JO ANN KARGUS 2017

Cardinals Hall of Fame

Branch Rickey ⚾ Chris Carpenter

Curt Flood ⚾ George Kissell ⚾ Lou Brock

Billy Southworth ⚾ Joe Medwick

Bob Forsch ⚾ Jack Buck ⚾ Stan Musial

August A. Busch Jr. ⚾ Jim Edmonds

Bob Gibson ⚾ Dizzy Dean ⚾ Willie McGee

Ozzie Smith ⚾ Red Schoendienst

Jim Bottomley ⚾ Chick Hafey ⚾ Bruce Sutter

Tony La Russa ⚾ Enos Slaughter

Marty Marion ⚾ Joe Torre ⚾ Ken Boyer

Pepper Martin ⚾ Frankie Frisch

Jesse Haines ⚾ Ted Simmons ⚾ Johnny Mize

Mark McGwire ⚾ Tim McCarver

Sam Breadon ⚾ Terry Moore ⚾ Mike Shannon

Rogers Hornsby ⚾ Whitey Herzog

WORLD CHAMPIONSHIP TROPHY
PRESENTED BY THE COMMISSIONER OF BASEBALL

©JOANN KARGUS 2017

11-TIME WORLD CHAMPS

St. Louis Cardinals™

St. Louis Cardinals

© JO ANN KARGUS
2017

WORLD

1926   1937   1934   1942

1944   1946   1964

1967   1982   2006   2011

SERIES

© JO ANN KARGUS 2017

THE MAHATMA

BRANCH RICKEY
VICE PRESIDENT

ST. LOUIS

HOF 1967

42

© JO ANN KARGUS
2017

Branch Rickey

DIZZY

HOF 1953

dizzy AND daffy

© JO ANN KARGUS 2017

Dizzy Dean

RED

Red Schoendienst
HOF 89

© JOANN KARGUS 2017

Red Schoendienst

LOU SPEED

LOU BROCK
892nd
STOLEN BASE
FIRST
INNING
TO TIE RECORD
BY TY COBB

BROCK
20

HOF 1985

© JOANN KARGUS 2017

Lou Brock

The Wizard
"Go Crazy Folks!!"
OPENING DAY BACKFLIP!!
Cardinals
1
O. SMITH
HOF 1985
2017
© JO ANN KARGUS
Ozzie Smith

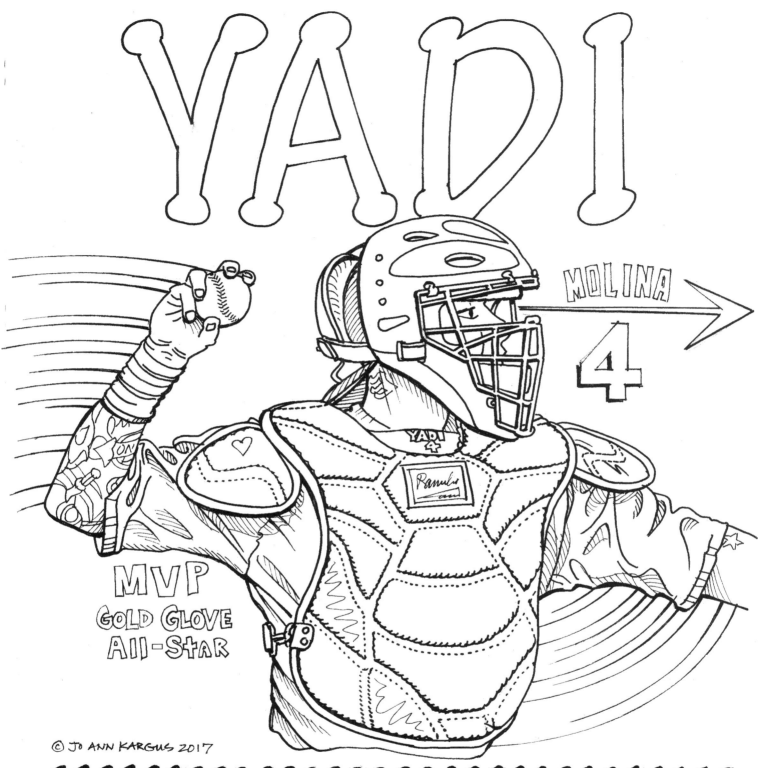

St. Louis RALLY

St. Louis CARDINALS

Cardinals

© Jo Ann Kargus 2017

Squirrel

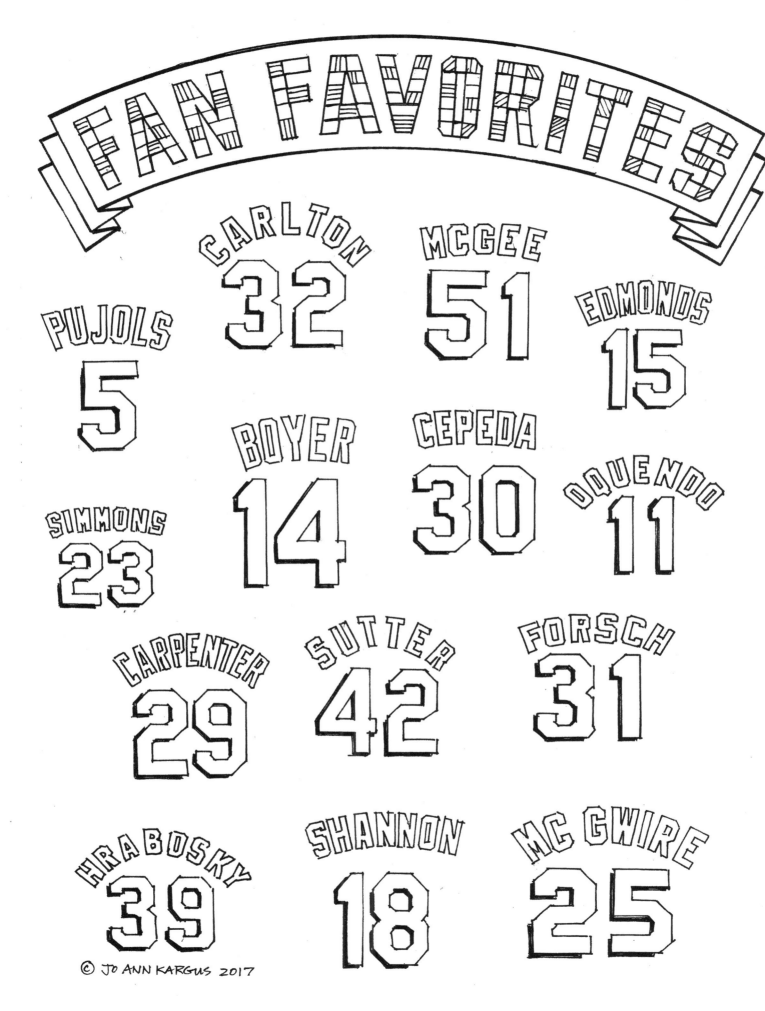

© JO ANN KARGUS 2017

OLE! OLE! EL BIRDOS!

St. Louis Cardinals

EL BIRDOS 1967

VIVA, EL CHAMPOS!!

El Birdos

1960s

© JoAnn Kargus 2017

Cards Win!

Game 5 of NLDS

WAINWRIGHT
50

YADI

© JO ANN KARGUS 2017

October 9, 2013

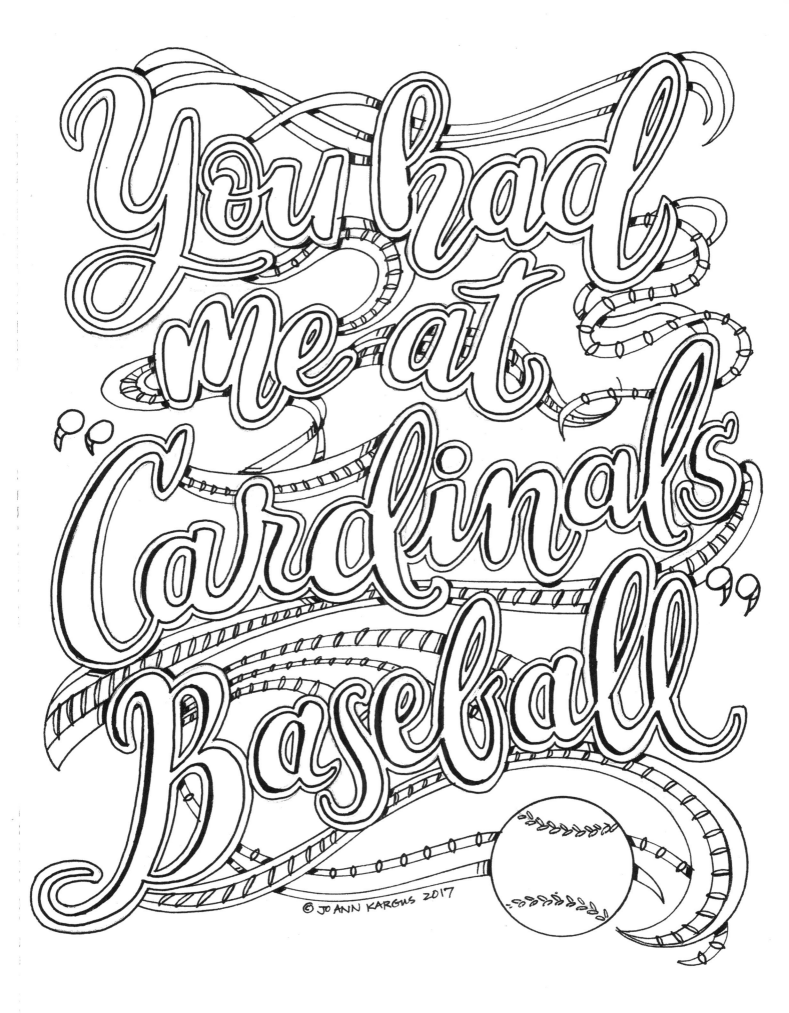

You had me at "Cardinals Baseball"

© JO ANN KARGUS 2017

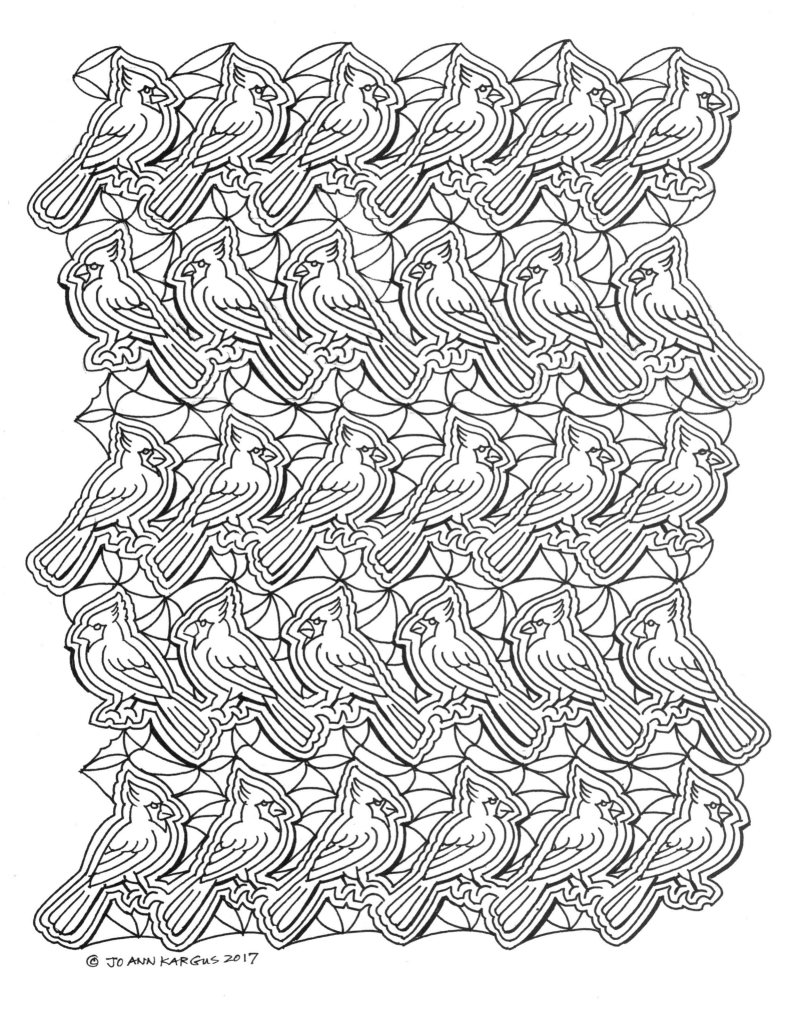

© JO ANN KARGUS 2017

Proud Member of Cardinals Nation

© JO ANN KARGUS 2017

The Cardinals of Cooperstown

Jake Beckley ⚾ Henry "Heine" Manush

Jim Bottomley ⚾ Joe Medwick ⚾ Orlando Cepeda

Charles Comiskey ⚾ Stan "The Man" Musial

Rick Ferrell ⚾ Roger Connor ⚾ Leo Durocher

Grover Cleveland Alexander ⚾ Enos Slaughter

Mordecai "Three Finger" Brown ⚾ Steve Carlton

Frankie Frisch ⚾ Pud Galvin ⚾ Rogers Hornsby

Rabbit Maranville ⚾ Dizzy Dean ⚾ Bob Gibson

Kid Nichols ⚾ Burleigh Grimes ⚾ Dennis Eckersley

Jesse "Pop" Haines ⚾ Cy Young ⚾ Lou Brock

George "Mule" Suttles ⚾ Leroy "Satchel" Paige

Vic Willis ⚾ Red Schoendienst ⚾ Ozzie Smith

Willie Wells ⚾ Bobby Wallace ⚾ Hoyt Wilhelm

Leon "Goose" Goslin ⚾ Johnny Mize ⚾ Dazzy Vance

© JO ANN
KARGUS
2017
Eddie Plank ⚾ James "Cool Papa" Bell

Chick Hafey ⚾ George Sisler ⚾ Bruce Sutter

Jesse "The Crab" Burkett ⚾ Rube Waddell

Celebrating 125 Years

© JO ANN KARGUS 2017

© JO ANN KARGUS 2017